Angelic Visitation

Fatima Abdulkareem

ISBN: 9798830534482

DEDICATION

This book is dedicated to God

CONTENTS

INTRODUCTION

For as long as I can remember, there was always conflict in my home. Not a few days passed by without Dad hitting Mum. My older brother and sister were not left out of his abuse. With the excuse of being a disciplinarian, he caned them for every little misdemeanor. I remember once, after another terrible episode that left him with bruises on his face, my brother told his friends and teachers in school the next day that he fell down the stairs at home; he was too embarrassed to tell them it was his dad who had beaten him so badly.

Fortunately, since we were much younger, my little sister and I suffered less in his hands at that time. It wasn't until a few years later when we were older, did we begin to have our share of beating. But even then, the emotional toll on us was no less traumatic.

One particular incident has stayed with me even to this day. It was the middle of the night, and I was fast asleep. I dreamt that Daddy was beating Mummy in our sitting room. Scared, I woke up sweating and quickly sat up in my bed. I strained my ears to listen for any noise, hoping it was all just a dream.

But it was not1. It was real!

I could hear Daddy shouting, followed by the sound of the belt lashing on flesh, and Mummy's voice crying out in pain each time the belt connected with her body. I got out of bed shaking, and in terror, tiptoed to the sitting room where the noise was coming from. What I saw will forever be etched in my memory.

I stood transfixed on the spot with terror as I watched Daddy hitting Mom just as I had seen in the dream. Mummy, now about seven months pregnant, was crouched behind a chair trying to hide from him with no success. He continued to deal blows to her with his belt until she was too weak to cry anymore. At six years old, I felt so small and helpless. 'Please stop,' I prayed silently, but he did not.

I could not take it anymore. I tiptoed back to my bed, hid under the covers, my whole body shaking, as I shut my eyes tightly against the tears that were already coursing down my cheeks, and covered my ears with my hands.

A week later, Mom delivered a frail, tiny baby girl.

The baby was premature. No surprises there.

Two years passed, but the beating had not stopped. It was now a daily occurrence, with Dad constantly getting drunk and venting it on Mummy. After a particularly nasty beating where she had been battered and had barely escaped with her life, she finally took up enough courage to run away.

I can never forget that day as long as I live. Everything that played out is still etched in my mind, as fresh today as it was some forty-something years ago.

I was asleep when I felt someone tapping me. I opened my eyes, to see Mom hovering over me. She put her index finger on her lips signaling for me to be quiet and then indicated that I follow her.

I knew at once something was up. Now alert, I jumped out of bed and stood beside her. With my almost two-and-a-half-year-old baby sister on her back, my younger sister in one hand and a small bag in the other, she tiptoed down the stairs while I followed, as we made for the door leading outside our house. Inside the small bag she carried, she had nothing except a few changes of clothes, her jewelry, and transport that would take us back to her parents' house.

Just as she opened the door and we all tiptoed outside, I heard shouting from behind me. It was my nosy aunt who happened to be around on a visit. She had seen mum sneaking off with us and alerted Dad. He caught up with us before we could make it outside the gate that would have led us to our freedom.

It was just before dawn, and still quite dark outside, but the uproar that followed woke up the whole street. Everyone on our street knew where the noise was coming from. My parents were the only ones in our posh neighborhood who fought almost every day. This morning was no exception, except that today, Mummy had made up her mind; she was leaving Dad.

Surprisingly, he did not try to stop her. He seemed almost relieved that she was going away. 'But only on one condition,' he told Mum. 'You can go away with the other two, but you must leave Fatou with me.'

Oh no! I groaned, why me?

It was true that I had a close relationship with my dad. Of all his children, I seemed to be his favorite and I loved him. But that feeling was tainted with fear of the man and hatred for how he treated Mum and his children. As young as I was, even I knew that, if there was going to be a separation between my parents, it was in my best interest to go with Mum.

But Dad would have none of it. Without even waiting for her response, he began to pull me away from her. I cried, begged, and struggled to be free to follow my mum, but he had his hands clamped on my arms refusing to allow me to go with her. Still, I wasn't about to go down without a fight. I continued to struggle to be free and, in the end, he had to physically drag me back into the house screaming and kicking, as he slammed the door against my mum. Next, he bundled me up the stairs, and back into the house.

I could hear mum's voice, shouting, 'Give me back my daughter,' as she continued to bang on the door but all her screams fell on deaf ears as Dad pushed me into his bedroom and locked the door, to make sure that I did not escape.

After a while, I became aware that I could no longer hear Mom's voice in between my sobs. The shouting had stopped and so had the banging on the door. Mum was gone with my two sisters and left only me behind.

I fell back on the bed and began to sob uncontrollably. To date, this day remains one of the darkest days of my life. I had just turned nine years and here I was already separated from my mother.

But the worst was yet to come.

Late one evening, barely a month after the ugly separation, Daddy told me to pack a few things. 'We are traveling tomorrow,' he said. He didn't tell me where we were going and I didn't ask. He was probably going on a business trip. And since I was too young to be left at home alone, he had decided to take me along.

As promised, we left early the next morning at dawn. The journey which seemed to go on forever was tiring and after a while, exhausted from all the excitement of travel I fell into a deep sleep.

I was awakened by a jolt, as the car bumped into something. As it turned out, after being on the road for many hours, Dad had turned into an untarred road full of potholes.

'Where are we going?' I wondered as the car continued to weave in and out of potholes on the dry dusty road. I tried to quell my curiosity, but still, I was getting uneasy. We had been on the road for more than six hours and we still hadn't arrived at our destination.

I didn't think a business trip should take this long.

I could see the sun going down as I looked through the car window. There was no way we could get back home today. Where would we sleep? I had so many questions going through my head, but I knew it was futile to ask Dad. He would not give me a direct answer. He could even get angry for disrupting his concentration. I had learned not to question him unless he chose to divulge information on an issue.

'Well, I will know soon enough,' I consoled myself and settled back in the back seat of the car.

It was almost ten minutes later when we finally arrived at a gate. Daddy promptly turned the car toward it and honked. It was opened by a lone man standing by whom, judging by his uniform, I assumed to be a security gateman. We drove into a large compound. I could see a big field and what looked like a block of classes as well as several other buildings of different sizes.

As we drove further in, I saw a few children milling around. They wore what seemed like uniforms. 'Why were we here?' I was getting worried again.

'Maybe Daddy came to see someone,' I thought. That was the

only explanation that made sense.

After another five minutes of driving, Dad finally stopped the car by one of the buildings. He told me to come down from the car while he went to the boot. At the same time, a woman came out and they exchanged pleasantries. From the way they greeted, it was clear they knew each other before now and that she had been expecting him. I looked up in confusion at my dad as he spoke to the woman wondering why he was holding my suitcase.

The next moment, Dad handed my suitcase to the woman and then turned to me.

"Fatou, this is your new school, he said. 'You'll be staying here from now on, okay?' He didn't wait for my reply but raised his hand to the woman with my suitcase, mumbling a parting greeting, he turned, quickly making his way back to his car. Before I could recover, he had already started the car. Waving to no one in particular, he drove off, leaving a cloud of dust behind him.

I stood there looking stunned. Where was he going? I asked myself stupidly. My brain was unable to process what was happening.

And then, slowly, it hit me. Dad was leaving me here!

But why? I wondered. 'Was he so desperate that Mum should not come back to get me that he had decided to take me so far away?' I wished he had told me of his plans. I could have tried to convince him not to send me away, which of course was why he had kept it a secret. Now it was too late. Hot tears spurted from my eyes, but he could not see them; he was gone.

I was to find out later that the reason Dad had so hastily sent me away to a boarding school in faraway Kwara State, almost seven hours journey from home, was not only because he did not want my mum to come back to get me but also, because he did not want me to be in the way of him and his new wife. He had been dating this woman for a while and was planning to bring her home. This was the reason he became even much meaner to Mum than usual and had seemed relieved when she said she was going away. Now that he succeeded in getting rid of Mum, nothing was stopping him from bringing his girlfriend home as his wife.

So, why hadn't he allowed me to go with Mum?

It just did not make sense. Why had he fought so hard to take me away from her when he knew that I would be a hindrance to his plans, or that he could not take care of me. As it turned out, I would have a reason, many times as I grew up, to ask this same question over and over again. For now, I felt lost. My world, which was shaky with my parents' constant fighting, had taken a turn for the worse because of the separation. And now, barely a month later, I had been sent away to a school far away from anything and anyone I had ever known.

Could anything be worse than this?

I hardly ever saw Daddy after that, except once or twice when he came for a visit to the school and on holidays. And after a while, He did not even come on visits anymore. On visiting days, every parent came to visit their child except mine. There was no guarantee that I would see him during the holidays either. At the end of the term, he would often ask my aunt, an uncle, or any of his friends that he could convince, to pick me up to spend the holidays with them, and to bring me back to school on resumption. It was obvious I was a burden to him.

LIFE IN MY NEW SCHOOL

Life in Iludun Oro Nursery and Primary school, as my new school was called, was tough. There was a matron an elderly woman, who oversaw all the hostels and ruled with an iron fist. Then there were the nannies who were directly in charge of the children. These were young women deployed to each of the three hostels. Their duties included taking care of the children while enforcing discipline and responsibility. 'Aunties,' as we called them, did not suffer fools gladly as any form of disobedience was met with immediate punishment. The daily routine was rigorous and rigid and mistakes were not an option. From a pampered sheltered albeit troubled life, I was suddenly plunged into a life of abandonment, loneliness, and hardship.

Still, I tried my best to adapt to my new school, doing my best to follow all the rules and regulations and avoid anything that would get me the cane.

But cane, I was soon to find out, was not the only threat in this school. There was another real threat to all the children, and that was hunger! Food portions were so small it was never enough for any of us. We were always hungry. When I newly arrived, I found most of the meals prepared so terrible that I could not eat them. But as time went on and the threat of starvation became real, I had to adapt. Even then, I was always hungrier, after every meal.

I became thin, weak, and very frail. So, frail that sometimes, teachers would exempt me from caning. 'Leave her o, before she faints in your hands,' one teacher said to the other, one day when I was about to be caned.

It was no surprise to anyone in the school, therefore, that shortly after, I fell seriously ill.

It started as a light cough. But as days went by the cough became increasingly intense. By the end of the second week, I had developed a fever, lost appetite, and become so weak that I could no longer attend classes. For the rest of the term, I was confined to bed. As I deteriorated, I became delirious and most times, was barely aware of my surroundings. The local doctors' prescriptions seemed not to be working and eventually each one had to confess that they were at a loss as to what was wrong with me. The school authorities became very worried and sent for my dad.

He never came. Not even when the term ended!

Instead, he asked one of his friends, Mr. Sule, to come and pick me up. I was to spend the summer holidays at his house. Since his daughter was also in my school, Mr. Sule picked up the two of us. I, however, had to be carried into the car since I could not walk.

Mr. Sule had not known that I was ill before picking me up from school. Dad had conveniently forgotten to mention it. However, on seeing how sick I was, he refused to keep me in his home. I only spent one night in his house. Early morning the next day, he chartered a taxi that would take me back to Lagos, straight home to my dad. He could not keep such a sick girl in his house, he said.

On arriving in Lagos, dad finally saw how critically ill I was and asked that my stepmom take me to the General hospital. After a series of tests, I was diagnosed with advanced whooping cough, severe malnutrition, and anemia. I was put under heavy antibiotics, multivitamins, iron tablets for blood, and several other medications. On the advice of the doctor, my dad interrogated me trying to find out the cause of my whooping cough. I told him how the food was always so small, and I was always hungry, and how our meals were usually prepared and served under extremely poor conditions. We were served on metal plates which were kept on the ground just outside the kitchen. By the time the school bell rang for us to go for our meal, the food was already cold and had been sniffed, slobbered, and sometimes, half-eaten by dogs and goats that usually hovered around. The cooks' half-hearted attempts to chase them away often yielded no result. The doctor said I must have been poisoned through the food from the school. He said I could very easily have died and that I was incredibly lucky indeed.

THE MIRACULOUS ESCAPE

This term, he had taken me to the market, bought lots of provisions for me, and taken me back to school himself. Upon arrival, he went straight to see the head of the school to lodge his complaint. He explained all that had happened to me during the holidays and how the doctor had said I could have died.

I was pleasantly surprised to find out thereafter, that a radical change had occurred in the school kitchen. The food was still in small portions but at least it was no longer kept on the floor. Now they were served from the pot, piping hot. It was obvious that the head of the school had talked with the cooks and kitchen attendants. Also, the cooks treated me more kindly, sometimes giving me a little extra portion of food. The news of my near-death experience had gone around the whole school. One staff member told me that they did not expect me back because the whole school thought I would die. Nobody had thought I could survive such an illness. It was, therefore, a miracle to see me back in school. Even the aunties eased up a little on the cane. At least for a brief time, I was a star of sorts and bathed in the glory.

But not long after, while still enjoying my newfound popularity in the school, I found myself in another trouble.

I was now in Primary four and Mr. Olu (not his real name) was our new class teacher. He was a mean man who took pleasure in beating children. His specialty was giving strokes of the cane on the buttocks. He did not have forgiveness in his dictionary. My classmates and I had suffered immeasurable cruelty from this man. Unfortunately, we could not report to anyone, not to our parents, or the authorities. In those days, children were to be seen and not heard. No one would have dared report an adult to another adult, even if they were the authorities. And so, we all continued suffering his daily beating, hoping to make the best out of it.

One day he called me to his table which was positioned in front of the class. 'Go to my house, 'he commanded, 'enter inside and you will see a Mathematics textbook on my table. Bring it to me quickly.' I rushed out of the class and began running to the staff quarters where he and other teachers of the school as well as a few other high-ranking staff lived. The staff quarters were far away from the academic area and located at the other end of the very big expanse of land that housed the school. It was quite a distance but I didn't mind. I was happy to be going on an errand for my teacher. Perhaps he would look at me more kindly, and I wouldn't be caned with the rest of the class today. Knowing Mr. Olu, I doubted it, but well, a girl could only hope' I thought, as I smiled to myself, hoping eagerly along.

As I approached the staff quarters, I could hear birds chirping loudly to themselves as they took shelter from the scorching sun among the tree branches. Apart from the birds, everywhere was eerily quiet.

The voices of teachers teaching and pupils that characterized the academic area had faded away. Here appeared to be a whole new world.

Despite the heat of the sun, I shivered a little unnerved by the almost eerie quiet. 'Thank God,' I whispered as I found Mr. Olu's house just ahead. I opened the door quickly, went in, and made straight for the table that he had mentioned.

Twenty minutes later, I was still going through the pile of books on Mr. Olu's table looking for the math book he had asked me to get for him. This was my third time checking through the books and I still couldn't find it. I was beginning to panic. I could see my teacher now, hand raised, cane in hand, about to hit me as I told him I couldn't find his book.

In fear of the dreaded cane, I made a renewed frantic effort to find the math book and began sorting through the pile of books again.

Just then, I heard footsteps on the porch. 'Oh dear, I hope that's not Mr. Olu.' Had he gotten tired of waiting for me to bring his book and decided to come to get it himself?

Suddenly the door was flung open and standing in the doorway was Mr. Olu. He stood in the doorway, blocking the sun with his short, stocky frame, hands-on-hips, a stern look on his face. My heart sank as I began to apologize. 'So sorry sir, I couldn't find the book. I've searched the table over and over again and . . ., 'my voice trailed off as he closed the door, and locked it with the key. Without saying a word, he put the key in the right pocket of his trousers and began to walk toward me.

What was he going to do with me? I wondered, scared out of my wits. There was no cane in his hands. Maybe he had a cane in the house and didn't need to bring one from the class. I looked at his face, trying to read his mood, but apart from the stern look, he gave nothing away.

What he did next gave me the greatest shock of my life. He quickly crossed the short distance between us and suddenly grabbed me by my thin shoulders.

Pulling me towards him, he began to fondle me.

'What was he doing?' I thought in panic. 'This was not how to punish a student?'

Oh my God! It suddenly dawned on me. 'Mr. Olu was not here for his book. He had other ideas. He had sent me here to molest me!'

He probably hadn't needed to get any math book in the first place. He had planned this whole thing all along.

As this realization dawned on me, a cold feeling of fear washed over me. I knew I was in real trouble. Terrified, I began to beg him, as tears formed in my eyes. 'Please sir, leave me alone. . . please, sir... I yanked myself out of his grasp and tried to run, but the room was small and he quickly got hold of me again.

He was the one pleading now; 'I will give you biscuits, sweets, pineapple...,' he said, trying to convince me with treats. As he held my two small hands down with one hand, he began pulling up my uniform with the other. I was squirming so much that he couldn't pin me down to carry out his evil act. But I couldn't get out of his grasp. 'Please sir, I don't want biscuits or pineapple or anything. Just let me go' I began to sob, frantically trying to get out of his grasp, but to no avail.

'This was it then,' I thought. 'I was about to be raped and there was nothing I could do about it. 'I had heard somewhere about girls who had been sexually molested but the whole concept had made no meaning to me. Now at just nine years old, I was going to find out firsthand. I thought of screaming but I knew it would be futile. Every student and staff were in a class by this time and the classes were so far away from the staff quarters that no matter how hard I screamed, nobody would ever hear me. We were not even on break yet so, there was no possibility of a roaming student or a teacher wandering around. Oh yes, Mr. Olu had this day so well planned.

But now he was trying to pull my uniform above my waist with one hand while still holding my two hands with the other and trying to pin me down with the weight of his body. I was squirming, trying to escape from him, at the same time sobbing and pleading for him to stop.

All of a sudden, as if in answer to my pleas, he stopped. I peered up cautiously at his face through my tears. It looked like one who had just woken up from a spell. On the spur of the moment, I quickly yanked my hands out of his grasp and realizing he was still holding my two hands in his, he released me and then, pushed me away. He quickly got up and without a word, walked towards the door, removed the key from his trouser pocket, unlocked the door, and walked out.

I ran to hide behind one of the only two chairs in the small room. I was confused. What did he go outside to do? Could it be to get a stick? That way he could cane me into submission. I wanted to run out through the door he had just left open but I was too scared. I stayed huddled behind the chair praying for divine intervention and waited. A few moments passed, and still no sign of Mr. Olu.

I came out of my hiding place and cautiously tiptoed out of the room onto the front porch, almost afraid that he would jump out at me any moment. I looked around but he was nowhere to be seen. I looked in the direction of the school area, and there was Mr. Olu in the distance walking quickly, probably going back to class. I could hardly believe my good fortune, I started back to class straightening my uniform and my hair as I went.

All the while, I was still in shock. 'What just happened?' I asked myself, still trying to grapple with the occurrence of a few minutes ago. 'Was I just almost raped?'

What had made him stop?

Perhaps he had heard the sound of someone coming. Or was it his conscience that had pricked him at the last moment? I doubted it. Mr. Olu had no conscience. Moreover, this was a premeditated assault, well planned. And the worst part was that he would have gotten away with his crime and no one would ever have been the wiser. I replayed the scene over and over again in my head. I could still feel his short meaty hands all over my body. I shivered again, from fear of what could so easily have happened to me.

I slowed down to a halt, as a thought occurred to me. What if he tried to make another attempt on me and I was not as lucky to get away as I was today? I was completely vulnerable. After all, he was my teacher and I could not refuse to go on his errand, even if it was a setup. Fresh worry began to form but I tried to brush it aside. God that had helped me today would still find a way of escape for me. So, thinking, my heart brightened a little as I continued my long walk to class.

In all of this, reporting to the head of the school or even a teacher never occurred to me. How would I ever live down the shame if anyone were to hear about it? First of all, nobody would believe that he didn't have his way with me. To be fair, if it hadn't happened to me, even I, naive as I used to be, wouldn't have believed the story that he decided to let go at the last minute.

And so, I told myself, telling anybody about this incident was never going to happen. My only prayer was that he would not make any other attempt after this.

He was already seated back at his table by the time I got back to class. As I entered, I saw him look at me from the corner of his eyes. He did not look up or challenge me as to where I had been or was coming from and I did not volunteer to give him any information.

Luckily for me, he never tried the sexual assault again. But then, he resorted to physical assault. For the rest of the term, Mr. Olu was in a rage, and he made sure the whole class knew it. He found every excuse to beat us. Twenty strokes of the cane and several in-between became a daily affair. He began coming to teach us during prep time too and sure enough, we got beaten before the end of the prep. Not surprisingly, I was the major target. He always found a reason to beat me or to increase my number of strokes when beating the whole class. And many times, for no just cause, he would single me out and give me strokes of the cane.

I didn't need anyone to tell me that Mr. Olu had decided to go on a revenge mission through physical assault since he wasn't able to have his way with me.

As the term came to an end, everyone sighed with relief that they'd be free from daily caning. We were all sore from the constant beating with most of us sporting bruises on our bodies. But unlike my classmates, I didn't feel relieved. I was worried. We were going on Easter break, a holiday that lasted only about two weeks. Before we knew it, we would be back in school. And I, for one, didn't think I would survive any more of the man's beatings

ANOTHER MIRACLE

I resolved to report my teacher's cruelty to my dad. Of course, I could never tell him about the rape attempt. I cringed, just thinking of anybody hearing about that. But I would tell him about the constant beatings and show him my scars

But Daddy was not the easiest person to talk to. You never knew what reaction to expect from him. So many times, I made attempts to speak to him but I couldn't summon up the courage. He and I were no longer close like before. The violent separation of him and Mum, with me in the middle of it all had created a kind of gulf between us. Being sent away to a school far away had not helped either. I no longer found it easy to talk to him like I had in the past. 'Moreover, I reasoned, 'how could I report my teacher's beatings to someone who himself was a wife-beater and a child beater.' Of course, Dad didn't see himself as a cruel man but fancied himself some kind of disciplinarian. I could imagine his answer as I reported my teacher to him... 'The best schools are those that enforce discipline,' he would reply, giving me a look of displeasure for even daring to report my teacher to him.

And so, I resorted to prayers. I prayed that God would somehow help me so that I wouldn't have to go back to that school. If he had saved me from sexual assault, surely, he could do this miracle too.

But alas, no such miracle took place. At resumption, Daddy told me to get myself ready to return to school. As usual, he didn't bother to take me himself. He had commissioned someone else to do the job for him. This time, it was a young man I barely knew whose friendship he had made while I was away at school the previous term. He was too busy to take me, he said.

Mr. Ejo, Daddy's new friend, did not have a car and we had to travel by bus. I cried all the way, throughout the seven hours journey to school, not even caring that we were in a public vehicle. Such was my dread of Mr. Olu.

We finally arrived late in the evening. I waved a limp goodbye to my travel guardian and slowly made my way back to my hostel. Each step I took seemed like I was walking to the hangman's noose. This was it then. Come Monday morning, we would resume the beatings and bullying where we left off the previous term. Fresh tears sprouted from my eyes and I began to cry again in self-pity as I began to unpack my things.

It was Monday morning.

The dreaded day had finally come and we were all waiting for our class teacher. Our class was the quietest in the whole school. You could hear a pin drop. You could feel the palpable fear throughout the class. Most of us had probably not had a good night's sleep. I knew I hadn't. Today we would know if the pattern of the last term was what we were going to follow or if our teacher had forgiven us. If not for the fact that I was so scared, that last part would almost have been funny. I couldn't imagine Mr. Olu forgiving anybody.

It was already past eight o'clock. Lessons were supposed to have started on the hour. I could hear the voices of other teachers in their classes already teaching. Where was our teacher?

The tension was killing me!

And then, suddenly, another teacher walked into the class. It was Mr. Dare (not his real name), the class teacher of class 4b.

'Mr. Olu is no longer in this school,' he went ahead to tell us. 'Till we get a new teacher, I will be the one taking your class and mine together.' He strode out quickly, the same way he had strode in. I was confused. I looked at the faces of the other pupils to know whether I had heard right. They looked as dazed as I was. Did he just say Mr. Olu was no longer in the school? No teacher had ever left the school before. Is this a trick?' I asked nobody in particular. I could hardly believe what I had just heard.

In all the time I was praying for God to intervene, it had never occurred to me to pray for my teacher to leave the school. In my mind, that had never been a possibility. This was an unexpected turn of events, a miracle to say the least. I concluded two things that day. One was that there was a God who answers prayers. And the second was that He answers in mysterious ways. Needless to say, my joy knew no bounds. Being free from the cruelty of our former teacher was the greatest gift my classmates and I could ever have imagined. That term was the happiest I had ever had in that school.

The rest of the time flew quickly by. Before I knew it, I was in class five, my final year. There was no class six and so, from here I was going straight to secondary school. We began to prepare for our entrance examinations, the requirement that would usher us into secondary school. The exams were rigorous but we had been well prepared by our class teacher. Luckily, till I left, there were no more incidents or distractions. I passed all my papers with flying colors.

I was admitted into the Federal Government Girls' College, Owerri in Imo State, one of the most prestigious secondary schools of those days. I was very happy, though a little anxious that the school was in faraway Owerri, Imo State. If Dad had found it difficult to visit me in a school seven hours from home, I knew it would be most unlikely he would visit me in a school almost twice the distance. So, I began to brace myself for the fact that Dad may never visit me at my new school. If I was lucky, he could come once. But better not to keep my hopes up to avoid disappointment.

I began to prepare for secondary school. A list of items to buy had been sent to us along with the admission letter. But things hadn't been going on well for Daddy on the financial front for some time now. We could only get a few of the things on the list; bucket, bed sheet, blanket, slippers, and a few essential toiletries. For provision, I had to make do with Garri (cassava flakes) and sugar. Things were really bad. As apprehensive as I was about going to a new school so far away, I couldn't wait to resume.

LIFE IN SECONDARY SCHOOL

Federal Government Girls' College, from the very first day, was challenging but interesting.

Daddy citing inadequate funds as an excuse had decided to put me on a bus going to Owerri all by myself. I didn't have the address of the school and even if I did, had no idea how to get there. And even if I did, he had given me just enough money to get a meal at the stopover. He didn't mention anything about how I would get to the school from the park and I didn't ask. It was around 6 am when we set out on the journey. As the bus began to move, Daddy was standing by my window, and told the woman sitting next to me, 'Please watch over my daughter.' And that was how I was left in the care of a total stranger, to go on a journey of over fifteen hours, to a place I had never been before, with no address and a very small amount of money. As God would have it, handing me over to that total stranger would eventually save me from being stranded.

Daddy's reassurance that we would get there around five pm in the evening of the same day proved false. We ended up spending over 20 hours on the road, eventually getting to

Owerri in the early morning the next day. It was almost 3.30 am the next morning when the driver finally maneuvered the bus onto the company terminus in Owerri and pulled over in the parking lot.

I got out of the bus with the rest of the passengers and went to locate my luggage.

On retrieving my suitcase from the bus, I went to stand by the side of a building which I assumed was their office. I hadn't the faintest idea what to do next. It was now getting to four o'clock in the morning but everywhere was still pitch dark. As I stood pondering what to do next, many questions began to flood my mind.

'How will I get to my new school?' I wondered. I didn't have directions on how to get there and I didn't even have the money to flag a cab that would take me there. I wondered, 'Would a taxi agree to stop for an eleven-year-old, standing alone, trying to flag a cab?' And what if he did stop and decided to carry me away to God knows where? All the stories of abduction, kidnappings, and murders I had heard about or watched in movies were often carried out on unsuspecting strangers.

Other morbid thoughts began to creep in unannounced. There were at least two hours more before dawn, where would I stay till then? Would I stand like this till the morning light? From where I was standing, I could see a group of touts eyeing me and talking in low tones among themselves. Were they talking about me seeing I seemed to be alone? What if they attacked me? As all these thoughts ran through my mind, I could sense the familiar feeling of fear beginning to claw at my belly.

Just then, the woman who sat beside me on the bus saw me

standing alone and came over. She had been looking for me everywhere, she said. She insisted that she take me to her house till the morning. 'I promise to take you to your school as soon as it is morning,' she said, as she saw I was hesitant. Anyway, I had no choice. It was either I go with her or fall into the hands of miscreants here in the garage. And so, I picked up my suitcase and bucket and followed her.

My benefactor was true to her word. We rested a few hours in her home, and as soon as it was daybreak, we boarded a taxi that took us straight to my school. At the gate, she introduced me to the gate attendants as a new student. The gate attendants checked their list of new students and upon verification that my name was on the list, promptly handed me over to a senior who took me to the authorities. By afternoon, that same day, I had been taken to my hostel, allotted a bed, and told what arm of class I would be receiving lectures from. I was also given a quick run-over of the rules and regulations of the school.

As I lay on my bed getting ready to sleep on my first day in secondary school, I went over all that had happened right from the day before when I boarded the bus to Owerri up until I arrived at my new school. I remembered how I would have been stranded if not for the kind woman who had taken it upon herself to help me. I was very conscious that I had been very lucky indeed. This trip could have so easily ended badly for me. I sighed with relief, thanking God for rescuing me once again from an impossible situation. Exhausted, I fell into a deep sleep.

 Life in secondary school was different from my primary school experience. There was a lot of discipline enforced in Federal Girls, as we fondly called it, but unlike Iludun-Oro, where 'aunties' rewarded breaking rules and regulations with the cane, here, the law of 'consequences of actions' were favored in place of the cane. Punishments, like cutting grass, cleaning toilets, sweeping classrooms, and so on, were usually meted out to erring students. Secondary school felt like freedom compared to where I was coming from. For a child who had been trained in a curtailed, almost military-like setting, this newfound freedom was almost scary.

In Iludun-oro, life had been strictly regimented. You were not given a chance to think for yourself. As long as you did what you were told you were fine. Falling out of line meant one thing, the cane. The school had structured it such that every waking moment was filled with an activity or a chore. There was usually no time for small talk or goofing around like kids usually do. I didn't have any real friends since the environment was not conducive to sustaining friendships. To be fair to the school, I guess they had to find a way to manage us since we were all so young. It couldn't have been easy to manage a school full of little children, some as young as four years old!

I guess you could say it was not surprising that by the time I got to Federal Girls, I found it difficult to relate to others. I had no idea how to make friends. Much as I wanted to interact with others and be accepted by them, I just didn't know how to go about it. I was suspicious of anyone that tried to get close to me and since I was always moody, no one wanted to come near me anyway.

My first few months were characterized by me being sad, and teary-eyed. I felt weak and sickly and sometimes couldn't go to classes. A kind senior took me to the school clinic which we called 'the sick bay' in those days. The nurses and the doctor had no idea what was wrong with me since I had no physical symptoms. There was no temperature, no headaches, nothing. But I was lean, very frail, not eating, and constantly crying. If it was now, the doctors would have quickly detected depression, but in those days, the concept was not popular, even in the medical field. And so, they did their best to manage the situation. They treated me for fever, gave me some antibiotics, and fussed over me. After weeks of fussing, I decided I was leaving the sick bay. I insisted that I was now okay. They discharged me.

I did my best to adjust. I went for classes, for meals, prep, hostel, doing all the normal things students do. But I felt estranged, undeserving, unworthy, like a misfit. Most of all, I felt so alone and abandoned.

It did not help that everybody seemed to have caring parents, who brought them to school when school resumed and visited them on visiting days. Even those, whose parents were in Lagos like me, managed to come to visit their children and wards. Parents, who were unable to come, sent provisions through an aunt, uncle, or older cousin. My dad never came to visit, not once throughout my six years in secondary school.

'I wish he had let me go with Mummy that day,' I thought for the umpteenth time. These days, I thought of Mum and my sisters all the time; even during classes. That was what I liked about Iludun. You weren't allowed to think, not with the rigid daily schedule and threat of cane constantly looming over our heads. But here, there was too much time to think. In between classes, during the break, before prep, after prep, weekends. . .

I wondered where they could be now. I knew for sure that if I had been with Mum, I wouldn't have gone through all the grief I had known. Certainly, I wouldn't have gone to a boarding primary school. I tried many times to ask Daddy where Mummy was, but I couldn't summon up the courage. His stance as a disciplinarian who did not tolerate misbehavior from children had taken new dimensions with him becoming even more tyrannical. I tried so hard to be a good girl but still got caned often. Even little offences were not overlooked. I was terrified of the man. And so, asking him about Mum face to face was out of it. I decided to write a letter to him from school. In the letter, I asked whether he had heard from Mum. I told him that I missed her terribly and would he please contact her for me?

I didn't expect him to reply. He usually ignored anything that had to do with a show of emotions. I was, therefore, very surprised when I received a reply to my letter. I was not to concern myself with such things as where my mum was, he said. Instead, I should focus on my schooling. 'The only thing you should be thinking about now is your studies,' he concluded.

 My last hope of reaching my mum had been dashed. That was the last card I played, and I had lost. Didn't this man know that the whereabouts of my mum and sisters were the only thing I ever thought about? That it was because of this very thing that I was slipping in my studies? I couldn't go on like this. At this rate, I didn't think I would make it through secondary school!

My art of daydreaming began one weekend in form two. It was a Saturday morning and I had finished my allotted hostel chores. Just across the long tennis court was a huge tree that had become a beehive of sorts for students. But this morning seeing that it was empty, I went to sit under the tree. It was a bit isolated from the hostel but from where I was, I could still see students going in and out of the hostel gate. Some could be seen standing in groups, gossiping. I began putting words together for my poem. I had a little jotter where I had written many poems. My poems were a lifesaver. They allowed me to put some of the things I felt on paper. This usually gave me some form of relief even if for a short while. After the reply from Dad about Mum, I needed to express myself. I began to write furiously on the jotter. I looked up again from what I was writing.

 What other words could I use to explain my grief? I decided to write a poem about Mum. Yes, that could calm me down. My mind wandered trying to remember some of our most memorable times together. One time she had dressed me and my sister up. As she tied each of our hair in colorful ribbons, she suddenly announced that we were going for an outing. And so, we did. She took us to the national theatre to watch a concert. Mum was like that. There was never a dull moment with her. A smile played around my lips as I remembered with nostalgia some of our fun activities together as a child.

I was rudely jolted from my daydreaming by the ringing of the school bell. It was time for lunch. A student rushed past me kicking up dust as she made her way towards the dining hall. I got up from the bench and began walking to the dining hall. Remembering my mum made me feel better, so much better in fact, that I was in a good mood the rest of the day. I felt so much happier than I had been for a long time.

That day, I realized that daydreaming was a possible escape tool for me, I began using it to make myself feel better, especially on days I was feeling really low. By the time I was in my third year, I had perfected the art of daydreaming so well that I was even able to deceive teachers. I appeared to be participating in class but was long gone in my world. No teacher ever caught me since I always appeared to be concentrating on what they were saying. I even joined in as the class laughed at a joke the teacher had made even though

I had no idea what the joke was. It was no surprise that I began to slip in my studies, slowly but surely, until finally, in my third year, my grades were so poor that I only barely got promoted to form four. Dad wrote to the school insisting that he was not satisfied with my result and that I had to repeat the class. To a girl whose self-esteem had already reached rock bottom, that was the ultimate humiliation. But I had no choice, and so I repeated.

SEEKING GOD

About the time I entered secondary school, I had begun to feel a strong pull to seek God. Even though I was just eleven years old, my young life had already been filled with major emotionally draining experiences. I had grown up witnessing almost daily fights between my parents, which eventually ended in an ugly separation. I was forcefully taken away from my mum and sisters due to the separation and barely one month later, I was taken away from all I had ever known and dumped in a boarding primary school far away from home and anyone familiar. I had been through a near-death experience, a near-rape attempt, and endured cruel beatings and treatments from both teachers and house matrons at school, and when at home, from my dad and later my stepmother.

And just recently, my father's best friend had taken to making advances on me. So far, he had not succeeded, but I didn't know for how long I could hold him off. He made sure to target when Dad was not home, which was often. To my young mind, telling Daddy was out of the question. I decided that the only thing to do was to continue to dodge the man anytime he came to our house. Thank God it was only when I came home for the holidays that I had to contend with him.

I had to wonder, was my life always going to be like this, always full of turbulence? I shuddered to think what would have befallen me if God had not saved me each time, I found myself in trouble. I decided to find out more about this God that had helped me thus far. I had a feeling I was going to need Him even more as I grew older.

I came from a Muslim home and had been taught about the tenets of Islam by my dad. But I felt that I needed to know more. And so, I went to the school library, trying to dig up any books I could find on Islam. After some research, I was able to dig up several Islamic books. Two of them in particular made an impression on me. In them, I learned so much more about Islam, the history, tenets and pillars, prayers, and so on. I devoured the books and began practicing all I read. I created a makeshift prayer mat and looked for a convenient, quiet place, and there I said my daily prayers, making sure to recite all the verses I had learned in my book. I found out that there were a few other Muslims in my new school and they had formed a club called the Muslim Students' Society, MSS for short. I enrolled and became an active member of the club. Indeed, by the time I was in the senior class, I was voted president of the club beating several other students to it. Some of the criteria used were attendance, dedication, and zeal, all of which I excelled in. I also took up Islamic studies as one of my subjects, paying keen attention to everything the teacher taught. I had become a devout Muslim scholar.

In 1985, I sat for and passed my West African Examinations Council (WAEC) with flying colors. That was a proud moment for me. Unfortunately, I wasn't able to get admission into a university until two years later. Since I was in between schools, I went to my hometown to stay for a while. Daddy had some projects going on there and I decided to follow him. It was here that I began to read books written by Islamic apologists. The purpose of these books was to discredit Christianity in its entirety proving once and for all that Islam was the only way to God. I read almost all the books. My favorite ones were those written by a man named Ahmed Deedat. Dad had imported the Islamic books in cartons. We often gave out the books free to anyone willing to read. We also used it to propagate Islam.

Encouraged by my interest in Islam, Dad joined forces with me and we began going out to evangelize. We started by giving the books to all the Christians in that area. We would then invite them to our house to watch Islamic videos in the hope of converting them to Islam. We made several good impressions and a few accepted Islam. Daddy had an open back range rover which we converted for evangelism. Daddy had an open-back Land rover that he drove around the town and with the aid of loudspeakers preached on the streets.

When we later went back to Lagos, Dad got an Islamic teacher for me and my siblings. After that, I got enrolled in a proper Islamic and Arabic college to learn the Arabic language. I was there for a few months when I received admission into the university to study Islamic Religious Studies with Arabic language as a minor.

But life at the university wasn't easy. Daddy had dated several women after Mum. The one that came in as soon as Mum left was long gone. After a long spell with a series of girlfriends, Dad finally decided to marry again. This one was a nurse and from the look of things, was here to stay. She had a very strong influence on Dad. Many said she used unorthodox means. Certainly, I had never seen Dad so tame, tolerant, and forgiving toward any of his wives. Alhaja was a party goer who went to night parties at will, often leaving Dad at home alone with us. On the day she didn't go to a party, she would say she was on night duty. After a few years, she became more and more brazen in her untoward attitude to Dad. She told him that she had been promoted and was now on permanent night duty. From then on, she hardly slept at home. She would come home, take a bath, change clothes and leave the house. We didn't see her again until the next morning. This became the new norm. Daddy didn't like it, but he did nothing. He had finally seen a woman who could tame him.

Things continued to degenerate. Dad's businesses had collapsed and he was almost always at home these days so much so that it became a struggle for him to even pay school fees. In addition, since Alhaja got to the scene, relations between Dad and me degenerated even further. He found fault in everything I did and took to hitting me for every perceived offence. Even though I was now 18 years old, that didn't stop Dad. It got so bad that I began hiding in my room. I noticed that he seemed to be more prone to being angry with me anytime Alhaja was around so I tried to please her so that I wouldn't get told on or beaten. I began to be afraid to go home and during the holidays would stay back in the hostel. After years of being in boarding schools, I had gotten used to being away from home and so now that I was older, and in the university, it was easy for me to stay back. With all the hostility I was receiving back at home, I felt it was better to stay away. He never reprimanded me for not coming home. I knew he was probably relieved that I didn't come home since he didn't have any money to give me for school fees or pocket money anyway. Most times, I survived on friends, and family, selling clothes and odd stuff in between to pay for my fees and make ends meet.

Earlier on in my second year at the university, I was kicked out of the hostel since I was no longer able to pay the hostel fees. I was forced to look for accommodation outside the school. The only room I could afford was in a ghetto, some distance from the school. It was in a block of rooms where the poorest of the poor stayed. We lived with goats, chickens, and dogs. There was usually little left for anything else after paying rent. I saw myself reliving Iludun, as hunger became a constant companion once again.

I wondered whether this was always to be the pattern of my life. I had tried so hard to be good, doing all that I knew to do as the Islamic tenets dictated, but I hadn't found relief or peace as I had hoped. Every step of my young life had been full of suffering, hardships, trials, and temptations.

Well, at least, God had helped me thus far in my academics. I was now getting toward the end of my final year at the university. I could not wait to finish my final exams. Then I would be able to get a job and be free from the constant lack of finance and helplessness.

A NEW PHASE

"'The Kingdom of God is at hand; give your life to Christ before it's too late.' That was one of my colleagues at my new office. Her name was Deola.

Since I resumed at this company, this woman had been badgering me with her born-again lectures. But she wasn't the only one. Several of her friends had also taken it upon themselves to engage me in their Christian persuasion. I often wondered how I got employed in this place full of born-again Christians, as they called themselves. From the Managing Director to the cleaner, everybody was a professing Christian.

I had never heard of the company before I got employed. A mutual friend who heard that I was looking for a job and happened to be working there had put up my name without my consultation. Since it was almost the deadline for the submission of the application, she had written the application on my behalf, submitted it, and contacted her friend to find a way of getting it across to me. They got across to me just in time for the interview the next day,

After several wrong turns, I finally located the company at the address given to me. But I was ill-prepared for what I would meet in the waiting room. I met several other people there already waiting to be interviewed for the same job. Everyone that applied already knew all about the company. They knew that it was owned by a Christian believer and that they only employed Christians. They had, therefore, prepared ahead. They all wore long flowing dresses or skirts, had no earrings, and had on weaved or plaited hair as was popular with the so-called 'Christian extremists.' Two of them even had scarves tied on their heads. I was the only odd one out, wearing a corporate skirt suit, earrings in my ears, my long hair tied into a bun, with make-up on.

One look at them and I knew this interview was not going to favor me. Not with my Muslim name, and certainly not with my certificate reading boldly, B.A. Islamic Studies. I felt a strong urge to forget the interview and leave, but still, I stayed.

I owed it to my friend who had gone to all that trouble to at least sit out the interview. Besides, I had gone through a lot of trouble to locate this place. The least I could do was to attend the interview even if only for the sake of formality. The interview itself went without a hitch. Still, I didn't expect any favorable response from them.

It was, therefore, with the greatest surprise that I received my letter of employment a week later from the company. They asked me to resume work at once. Apart from the cleaner, I was the only Muslim in that organization. And till I left; they never employed any other Muslim.

'I'm telling you; Jesus is the only way, the truth, and the life. . . 'The voice of my new office mate Deola, startled me out of my thoughts. I was beginning to get irritated by her constant harassment. Since I had resumed work here a month ago, hardly a day passed without her preaching to me. Initially, I masked my irritation behind smiles hoping she would finally give up and leave me alone, but she was getting more determined by the day. I decided to put Deola and her fellow preachers in their place once and for all. I was through with being nice. By the time I was done with them, they would never bother me again.

Today I would crush their little ideologies about their beloved Jesus and let them know how misguided they were about the real truth. After all, I hadn't been an Islamic scholar almost all my life for nothing. I knew all there was to know about these matters.

'First of all, Deola,' I started, 'it is blasphemous to call Jesus the Son of God or God. He was just a prophet like any other prophet. Why would you say that it is through a man that we can make heaven? You guys are just deluded. . .' I went ahead to download all that I had been taught for so many years about the Christian religion, ending with the fact that it was because Christianity had become a religion of idolatry that God sent Prophet Muhammad with the Islamic religion to correct this anomaly. My arguments were superior, well researched, and delivered. In the end, none of them could win an argument against me, they left me alone. I had successfully defended the Islamic religion. I had won. Nobody disturbed me anymore with their preaching after that argument except Deola. And even hers were half-hearted attempts which she finally gave up when she noticed how unreceptive I was to any more of her preaching.

Now that nobody bothered me anymore, I was free to do my work. After all, wasn't that what I came here for, to work and get paid?

But God wasn't done with me yet.

Every morning, we had one-hour-long prayers before the start of business. Since everyone knew my stance, nobody called me into the prayer meeting. I could hear them seated at my post as a receptionist by the door. One thing, however, baffled me about these people. For one, I couldn't understand why they needed to take a whole hour just to pray. Not only were the prayers so loud, but it was always so passionate and emotional. Sometimes, it felt like they were seeing who they were talking to.

This morning I could hear some of them speaking gibberish. Some were even crying. 'What was making them cry?' I wondered. Were they not embarrassed crying in an office environment, making all this noise in the name of praying?' But they seemed not to care about anyone or anything else during the prayer session.

After prayers, everybody went about their normal duties like nothing had happened. The next morning, they would meet again together for prayers. Same pattern, loud prayers, tears, gibberish, and so on. I didn't think I was going to be able to stay here long. All this Christian emotion and fanaticism was getting on my nerves.

But I stayed, for the next three years at least. There were several good reasons for this.

First, I noticed that despite my stance on my religion, nobody discriminated against me. I was treated the same as any other staff. Despite being a company built on strong Christian values, nobody tried to bully me or treat me differently in any way.

And then, there were the incredible acts of kindness and love. Here, people treated each other with respect and kindness. They did things for each other, covered each other's weaknesses, and helped to elevate each other. There was just so much love coming from everyone. Bosses treated lower-ranking staff with respect and consideration. Everyone had equal opportunities to grow in the company. We were like a family, loving, protective, and always supporting each other.

The type of family I never had.

And so, I stayed. Thank God the prayers were only in the morning. That was a price I was willing to pay to stay within such a loving environment.

Three years later, I decided to leave the company. Another company had given me a better offer with a higher salary. I opted to go take up the offer. I would be leaving Regency finally with their early morning prayers and spirituality. Not that I minded. By this time, I was already used to it. But well, greener pastures called.

Unfortunately, the job fell apart. I was to find out that the owner of the company was dealing in fraudulent businesses which could even have implicated his staff. I wasn't ready to be involved in any legal issues with unsatisfied customers. I quit the job.

For the next two years, I was between jobs. But I was in no particular hurry to get another one. I had taken up a small pottery business. I had also written a book which I displayed for sale in bookshops. Sales from my book were not yet coming in as expected, but I was hopeful. On the spiritual front, however, I wasn't doing too well. I still carried out the tenets of my religion, but for some strange reason, I wasn't fulfilled. The love and kindness I had experienced in my former company kept coming back to me. I was living in a rented apartment with my sister, my cousin, and a family friend and we were quite close, doing almost everything together. Where then was this feeling of loneliness coming from?

MY CONVERSION

42

I sat on my mat, rounding off my morning prayers.

Suddenly, images of morning prayers in my former company drifted unannounced into my mind. I remembered how they prayed with so much feeling and depth, giving themselves freely to their emotions, not minding who saw them or could hear them. These were not prayers from chapters memorized and recited to fulfill a religious obligation and make one free from guilt. No, these were prayers that came from hearts that were willingly loyal to their Maker. It was obvious that there was a loving and close relationship between them and this God they served. I was forced to admit that I missed Regency. I missed the atmosphere of love, acceptance, and kindness. Strangely enough, I especially missed the morning prayers. Even though I hadn't taken an active part in the prayers and religious activities, I had felt like a part of the bond. I could see them now, talking about God with such excitement, praying to Him like He was right there with them, afterward, going about their work with smiles, radiating an inner glow. These people always seemed to know something that I didn't. I wish I could experience, just once, whatever it was that seemed to always make them happy

'But how? I wondered. I wasn't ready to give up my religion. Islam made sense, was organized, and safe. All you needed was to observe the five pillars and do good deeds and you were likely to make heaven. 'Maybe if I tried to do more good deeds, I would feel better.' I had been a model child growing up, always trying to avoid trouble, always quick to do what I was told. I hadn't changed. But maybe I needed to do more good deeds. Yes, I was going to try to show more love and be godlier. I was determined to prove to myself that the holiness, righteousness, and love they preached could also be practiced in Islam.

After several months of renewed acts of love and kindness, a more intense dedication to prayers, and desperate attempts to attain a state of righteousness I gave up. Nothing had changed. My heart was still so heavy, tormented even. 'Why was it so hard to attain the peace and joy I yearned for?' I asked myself. My past haunted me. My future seemed bleak. 'Oh God,' I prayed desperately one morning, 'all I want is to be at peace with You and to be assured that I will be with You in Heaven on the last day. Show me the path You want me to follow'. And then I said something so radical that it could have been termed a blasphemy. I told God, 'If you refuse to show me the way, it would not be my fault that I made the wrong choice. You will be the one to take the blame on the Day of Judgment.' I guess I had almost overdone it, but as I said, I had gotten desperate and I meant every word of it.

A few weeks later, one of my old friends came to visit me. We had worked together in Regency before I resigned. He happened to live down the road, a few blocks from my house, and came once in a while to find out how I was doing. As was his custom, he began preaching again urging me to give my life to Christ, insisting that Jesus shed His blood for me to cleanse me of all my sins. 'Why are you always talking of sin?' I blurted out in irritation. 'By any standards, I'm a good person. I love God and have always tried to avoid what God frowns on to maintain good standing with Him. Why do I still need Jesus' blood to wash away my sins as if I was a murderer or someone evil?' His reply shocked me. He said, 'It is written in the Bible that: 'All our righteousness is like filthy rags. This,' he continued, 'means that no matter how good you think you are, you can never be righteous enough for God because you cannot meet His standards of holiness.' He concluded by insisting that the only way I could be sure of being free of sin was if God Himself cleansed me by the provision He made available to me through the blood of Jesus.

That one hit me hard. Over several weeks, I pondered on it, examining it from different angles. Finally, I had to conclude that it made sense. Who was I to think that I could be good enough for God? I agreed that God's standard of righteousness was way beyond what I could ever attain. I didn't have what it took to maintain it. I remembered the many times I had tried to stop myself from falling into error and still fell anyway. I cringed as I remembered some of the lies, I had told, some people I was yet to forgive, times I had gotten angry, backbiting, slander, bad thoughts. . . I sighed. I was not as good as I had thought, after all.

One month later, I finally gave my life to Christ.

But I was too shy to do it publicly. And so, I called my old friends from Regency. Four of them came, including the one that lived down my street. And yes, you guessed right. Deola, my friend, the relentless preacher was among them! They gathered around me and led me as I prayed the sinner's prayers. I had become a born-again Christian! They encouraged me to join a Bible-believing church, which I did. There, I went through the foundational classes and then the baptismal classes. By the end of the year, I was baptized.

45

THE REVELATIONS BEGIN

Life as a born-again Christian was pretty much the same. I ate, drank, worked, slept, and woke up the same. Everything appeared to be normal. Nothing extraordinary had happened in my life so far. Well not visibly anyway. But inwardly, I felt a sense of peace that I had never felt in my life. I had a sense of being where I was supposed to be. There was a strong conviction in my heart that I had done the right thing. I knew without a doubt there was no going back.

Two years after I gave my life to Christ, I began to have revelations from God. They came in the form of dreams. I have decided to share four of the most profound of them all.

1st Revelation – The Confirmation

The very first revelation came as a spiritual interpretation and confirmation of what I had done by becoming a follower of Christ. It went as follows:

I was in a dream, but it looked very real. It was a normal day like any other. The early afternoon sun was just beginning to make its way through the clear blue skies. I could tell it was going to be a beautiful day. I stood outside, watching people all over the earth as they went about their normal duties. For some reason, I could see the whole world from where I was standing, and this didn't appear strange at all.

Without any warning, the weather began to change, and everywhere suddenly became dark. The air felt heavy like when a bad storm is threatening. This happened all over the world simultaneously. Instinctively, I looked up, noticing that the once clear blue sky had become dark, and ominous.

Something was making its way through the dark cloud towards us. Initially, I couldn't make much of it, but as it cut through the skies and began descending to the earth, I saw that it was an aircraft of sorts, except it was much bigger. Indeed, it looked more like a spaceship. Soon enough, it landed on the ground not too far from where I was standing. Certainly, this was the biggest aircraft I had ever seen in my life. I couldn't see anybody driving the ship. It seemed to be an intelligent entity on its own. With a knowing that only comes in dreams, I realized that the end of the world had come and that the huge spaceship had come to carry people from the earth. I saw people running helter-skelter. There was panic everywhere.

Before I knew what was happening, I found myself on the ship, but I was not the only one. There were at least hundreds of thousands of us on that ship. I sighed with relief knowing that I was going to Heaven. The ship had come to carry the saints back and thank God I was among them.

At least so I thought.

I felt a slight jolt as the ship began to move, but rather than take off into the skies as I had thought it would, it did quite the opposite. The ground on which it had landed just moments before opened up right under us and we began to descend into the deep dark pit below at a great speed.

Then it dawned on me, that we *were not going to Heaven as I had previously thought.*

We were going to hell!

Fear gripped me upon the realization that I was going to a terrible place of no return and there wasn't a single thing I could do about it? How had this happened?

I had always been so religious.

I looked around trying to see if there was anyone who could help me make sense of what was happening, but they all seemed to be just as confused and panicked as I was. The fear on their faces was enough to tell me that I was not going to get any help there. This journey it seemed was going to be everyone for himself. Till today I always struggle to find the right words to explain what I went through in that experience. The sense of helplessness, hopelessness, and despair that hit me is beyond description. I was like a condemned criminal being taken to prison. Except this was much worse, I was going to hell, for eternity, and I was terrified!

It is worth mentioning that not once in the entire vision did, I remember anyone that I knew on earth. Not my parents, not my friends, not even my husband or my children.

Indeed, the most profound message I took away from that experience is that each of us is on an individual journey. We came to this earth alone and we will go back alone. Any relationship on earth is either for the purpose of interaction or propagating the human race or both. In the end, we will each go back to answer the One who sent us here.

The question is, which ship will you go back in? The one going up into Heaven or the one going down into the pit of Hell?

As I discovered, it is a choice each of us has to make alone!

As for me, my day of reckoning was here and I had failed. And now I was on my way to hell.

But thank God for His divine mercy and intervention

We must have traveled through that dark pit for like thirty minutes by earth's timing when without any warning, a brilliant light infiltrated the darkness in the ship. I looked up towards where the light was coming from and saw it was emanating from an angel. The angel was standing at the edge of the pit from where the earth had opened up and the ship had descended about half an hour ago. I seemed to be the only one aware of this light because no other person looked up, nor did they appear to notice the angel. Because we were so far away, I couldn't see his features except that he was wearing a flowing white robe and the light emanating from him was so bright. Still, I saw him bending into the pit as he called out to me in a loud voice, 'Shout the name of Jesus!' Without thinking twice and without hesitation, I shouted with all my might, 'JE-E-S-U-US.'

Then the most incredible thing happened. The ship that had been spiraling downwards at an incredible speed into the dark pit, stopped.

And with the same speed, it had descended, it began to move back upwards.

Before I had time to think about what was going on, it got back to the earth and once again without taking a step, I found myself out of the ship, back to where I was standing before I was picked up. I was the only one who saw the light, and the angel, I was the only one who shouted *Jesus*, and I was the only one the ship dropped off on the earth. Without a moment's delay, still, at that same speed, it descended back into the pit carrying the rest of the people with it.

And then the earth closed up as if nothing had happened.

As you can imagine, I was swamped in fear. I could not believe that I had just been delivered from going to hell. Still shaken, but full of relief, I began to thank God for saving me from going to hell.

And then, I woke up. I was sweating, my heart pounding. It took me a while to realize I had been in a dream. It was all so real.

For days after, I walked around as if in a bubble. I wondered, 'so this is how I would have gone to hell.'

I was so glad that I had given my life to Christ. And then it also hit me, this is how so many are going to end up in hell.

People encounter Jesus every day, either through someone preaching on the streets, on TV, one on one evangelism, or through books, pamphlets, and so on. But many choose to ignore these messages. We're either too busy or uninterested. While some like I did have closed their ears to any other message. They have their own opinion of what it takes to get to heaven because of their religion and are not ready to entertain any other opinion. Unfortunately, religion cannot save you. Only accepting Jesus as your Lord and Saviour can. And just as I saw in the dream when the end comes, there will be no warning. Everything will happen in a split second and there will be no time to make amends. I pray you will not remain stubborn to the end; it will simply be too late!

2nd Revelation-Heavenly Consecration

This one happened a few months after the first revelation. As I slept, I found myself in a dream walking in the afternoon along a major road that leads to the market in my area. All of a sudden, I saw myself falling under an overwhelming force. I could do nothing to prevent the fall. I lay there on the road and then, a fog came over me and enveloped me. People were going about their normal duties. They appeared not to notice me as they passed by my semi-conscious body on the ground. I was not conscious of time either but I guess I must have lain down on the ground in that fog for many hours. Moments after the fall, I saw an angel coming toward me. I could see him through the fog. The next moment, another angel came out of nowhere and chased the first angel away. I noticed she was a woman. The first angel changed and I saw it was the devil masquerading as an angel. Since he had been exposed, he didn't bother to hide his intentions anymore but began throwing different things at me. In the realm of the spirit, those things represented tragedies, sorrow, sufferings, trials, and tribulations which were meant to befall me. But the real angel did not allow any of it to get to me. The devil kept trying to throw these things at me, but each time, the angel would deflect them from me with her hands. This continued for a while. Finally, he got tired and left after which the fog was lifted and I stood up from the ground where I had lain for hours. By now it was night. Thereafter, I saw myself with tracts in hand, giving to people. In those tracts were written gospel messages for them to give their life to Jesus.

I woke up.

Initially, I was very confused by this dream, but the Holy Spirit gave me the interpretation.

He showed me the portion of the Bible where Jesus was led into the wilderness. After forty days of fasting, the devil came to tempt him but he did not fall into that temptation. The Bible says, '*After that, the angels came to attend to Him.*'

The Holy Spirit had slain me in the spirit and delivered me from the plans of the devil while anointing me in preparation for my ministry!

3rd Revelation- Judgment Day

I was in a vision and suddenly I saw myself before the Lord. While still in the dream, I began praying, 'Oh God, the wickedness on the earth is too much.' Why don't You bring the world to an end so that all the evil will stop?' As soon as I finished the prayer, I saw the judgment seat of God appear with the Father Himself seated on the throne. The whole earth got dark and instinctively everyone knew the world had come to an end! There was panic everywhere. People could be seen running around. Some were looking for their loved ones, some trying to get home, and so on. However, there were a handful of people scattered here and there who seemed not to be panicking like others. This set of people was dressed in very beautiful apparel. They seemed happy and were smiling as they appeared to be waiting eagerly for the judgment to begin. When I woke up from that dream, I realized more than ever, how close we are to the end. God was telling me that if the world were to end today, many are still not ready.

I want to use this opportunity to beseech anyone reading this right now. It is not a coincidence that you came across this book. It is part of the plan of God to reach out to you. You need to give your life to Jesus. Tomorrow may be too late. My dear brothers and sisters, heaven is real and so is hell. No more dilly-dallying. You've got to make up your mind. NOW! God bless you as you yield to what the Spirit is saying. Amen

As for you who once knew the Lord but for whatever reason have strayed away from Him. It is because He loves you that He has made this opportunity available for you to repent and rededicate your life back to Him. On the last day, no excuse will be enough to justify yourself.

Let us all keep in mind that there is a day of judgment for us all. You cannot use your father or mother, husband or wife or children as an excuse. So many trials and tribulations are not an excuse. Life has been so hard, will not hold water. I was always so busy trying to make ends meet, will not count. I tried hard to be good, will not make it. The only question will be, 'Did you KNOW the Lord Jesus Christ as your personal Saviour and Lord?' Please take note of the emphasis on KNOW. This is because you may give your life to Him and still not know Him. Knowing Him means that after saying the salvation prayer that makes you born again, you take time to walk with Him, be close to Him and be obedient to His word. Without that, on the last day, you will be one of those whom Jesus spoke of when he said, 'Go away from me, for I do not know you.'

Reading this book has enabled you to encounter Jesus. My prayer for you is that you yield to what the Spirit is saying by surrendering your life to Him just like I did many years ago. AMEN

4thRevelation-The Strange Dream

I saw the skies becoming dark with sounds of thunder and lightning as if it was about to rain. But instead of rain, I saw some things falling from the skies and landing on the earth. They looked like stars but I couldn't be sure exactly what they were. As they fell, terrible occurrences began to take place. I saw earthquakes, volcanoes, houses burning, all sorts of accidents, and other calamities taking place in every part of the world. There were a lot of dead bodies on the ground. And then the stars or whatever they were that had fallen on the earth got up and entered into the dead bodies. Immediately, the dead bodies came alive and began to move around. But the spirit inside them was no longer of the original owners of the body. This was the evil spirit that had fallen from the sky. The mission of the spirit was to destroy everyone on the face of the earth. Seeing them you would not know because they appeared like normal human beings. The only reason I knew was because God had opened my eyes to identify them in the realm of the spirit, and even I was almost deceived once or twice.

Now, all they had to do was to go close enough to somebody and the spirit of death would be transferred to that person. He would die and the next moment would rise again with the new spirit and start going about normally but now with the spirit of death. If he came in close contact with someone the person would die, rise again and go to infect someone else. And so, it continued until the number of walking corpses as I call them began to multiply over the face of the earth. In that dream, they tried several times to infect me, but because I was able to identify them, with the help of God, who had to carry me over sometimes, they never got me.

However, as I kept running to avoid them, I noticed something peculiar and strange. Under tents and gatherings, Christian believers were praying profusely, praising God, and worshipping. The walking corpses never went to them to infect them. They avoided anywhere they saw believers gathered together praying. It didn't occur to me to go into any of the gatherings. Instead, I kept running from them until I ran into a room and shut the door against them. I waited to see whether they would still be able to come in, but they couldn't.

I was safe, they hadn't got me.

I had this strange dream over ten years ago and for a long time, it confused me. It was the most confusing dream I ever had. I didn't understand it and couldn't decode it. I told a few people who I knew were good at interpreting dreams. They were just as confused as I was. I concluded that maybe God was trying to show me something that was going to happen in the future. That seemed like the only logical explanation.

Fast forward to the year 2020. One day during the heat of the coronavirus pandemic, my husband reminded me of the dream. Initially, I couldn't even understand which of the dreams he was talking about since I had had several notable ones. But he pointed out to me that it was the one with the dead bodies, explaining that some of the details sounded like what I said I saw in the dream. For example, where I said that if one of the beings came close to a normal person they would be infected and die. Is the coronavirus not transferred by infected people coming close to another person? he asked. 'Also, you said that you became safe when you got into a room and closed the door. Does that not sound similar to staying at home during the lockdown?' He asked.

'Yes, the dream seemed to have several connections with the pandemic,' I replied.

 It could very well be that God was giving me the spiritual overview of how coronavirus was to come on the whole world. Oh well! As I said, it was a strange dream.

TESTIMONY TIME

Truth be told, my life has become one of everyday testimonies. When I was a new convert, I thought the born-again Christians were trying to brag to make them appear holier than they were. Some of the testimonies I heard sounded so out of this world, that I couldn't believe they were real. That is until I began to have testimonies of my own. There are so many that I can't begin to count them. But here I will mention just two of them.

1st Testimony- My son's healing

He had been stooling frequently for days now. Three days earlier, as I changed his nappy, I noticed that his stool was a little watery, greenish, and smelly. 'Not so soon,' I sighed. These were typical signs of teething in babies. I remembered when my first child was about five months old and I noticed these same symptoms. I rushed him to the hospital, only to be told that when babies were preparing their teeth, they sometimes showed some symptoms like watery stool, loss of appetite, and high temperature. They had sent me off with something to help bring down the temperature. 'All this will go away once the teeth start coming out.' The doctor told me.

And so, it was. At six months, the first sign of a tooth began to appear, and true to what the doctor had said, all the symptoms gradually disappeared.

This particular baby was starting on his own earlier at four months, but I was reassured by my experience with my first child and didn't immediately panic as I had done the first time.

But that was, until the second day when I noticed that the stooling had become even more watery and more frequent. Also, his appetite had greatly reduced and he had a little fever. I told my husband the situation when he came back from work and we decided to buy the drug that the doctor had prescribed for my first son a year earlier. But when we got to the pharmacy, we found out that the price of the drug had increased and we didn't have enough money to buy it. We were a young couple and, in those days, we were not so financially buoyant, nevertheless, my husband promised to source the money when he went out the next day.

Unfortunately, by the next day, the boy's condition had grown worse. He refused to take anything today, even breast milk, his absolute favorite. Because he refused to eat anything, he was passing out only a watery stool. His pale body showed he was getting dehydrated. By noon, he had become so weak that his eyes were drooping. I could feel him becoming limp in my arms.

I tried to shake him awake but there was no response. The only thing that reassured me he was alive was his breathing. I began to panic.

'What was I going to do?' I paced up and down our small bedroom with my baby in my arms trying to think. My husband was away at work. There was no way to call him as there were no handheld phones in those days. He had promised to get some money to buy the drugs on his way home, but that was hours away. This child needed attention now. This child wasn't going to make it till evening. 'What will I do now?' Tears began to well in my eyes.

Suddenly, I heard a voice. It said, 'Pray!'

Without thinking, I began to strip my baby of all his clothes. Quickly, I removed everything on him, including the nappy, and lifted him in my hands. As I raised his almost lifeless body, I saw myself setting him at the feet of Jesus who was seated on His throne. I began to speak. I said, 'Lord, you know that I did not ask for this child. He came in unannounced when I least expected him. Because of this, I know that You brought this child into this world for a great purpose. Lord, I have laid him at Your feet, naked as he came into this world. You alone have the power to heal Him. We have no money to buy drugs for him but I trust that You can heal him, Lord.' After the prayers, I dressed him up again in his clothes.

A few moments after the prayers, the first thing I noticed was that he opened his eyes. The next moment, he agreed to eat. The third miracle was that after about ten minutes, he pooped in his nappy. Upon checking, I found the stool was no longer watery but formed.

By the evening of the same day, the watery stool, fever, loss of appetite, and every other symptom that had plagued the boy for three days had completely disappeared. Just like that. My baby was completely healed and was back to his normal active and energetic self. His first tooth came out unannounced, a month later. Furthermore, till all his baby teeth came out, there were no more symptoms whatsoever. Praise the Lord!

Till today, I don't know what made me do what I did but as I grew older in Christ, I came to understand that the Lord leads us by Himself to do certain things when He wants to do a miracle in our lives. My natural self would never have stripped my baby naked, but thank God I didn't listen to my natural voice. I yielded to the voice of the Holy Spirit and He brought about a great healing miracle in my baby's life.

2nd Testimony- Family Planning Gone Wrong

Toward the end of 2011, I went to the family planning clinic for a check-up on the option that I had installed. It was a routine check-up just to make sure that the coil had not shifted and that there was no infection. Usually, it didn't take more than ten minutes for the nurses to check me and certify that everything was okay.

But today was not like other days. Upon checking me, the nurses declared that they could not find the coil. Every effort to locate it proved abortive. They referred me to the general hospital. At the hospital, the nurses also tried without success to find the coil. They referred me to a lab for a scan.

When the scan result came out, it was discovered that the coil had shifted and was now placed in an awkward position against my womb. There was no way to get there except by surgery.

I could not believe my eyes. How did I go from just going for a routine check-up in the morning to preparing for surgery a few hours later?

My name, weight, age, and other such details were documented. I was given a date to come back for the surgery.

It was not something they could do immediately, they explained, since it was major surgery and they would need to prepare for it.

I left the hospital with a heavy heart. I called my husband and gave him the news.

'How was I going to get out of this one,' I wondered. I had always believed that with God, there was always a way out of every situation, but even I was not optimistic about this one. Two obvious facts buffeted my faith and made it impossible to hope. First was the fact that the coil was missing, and the second was that they had found it through the scan lodged inside my womb, out of reach, except by surgery.

What do you do in a hopeless situation?

Well, I did the only thing I knew to do. Go to God. I began to pray, 'Heavenly Father, I come before You. Even in this seemingly hopeless situation, I know you are still God. Lord, I don't know how, but I know that only You can turn around this situation because You said that You will turn things around for good for me. You also said that You will make a way where there seems to be no way.

'I stand by Your word which says, "With man it is impossible, but with God, all things are possible." Lord, I have no idea what You are going to do or how You are going to do it. All I ask is Your divine intervention in this matter.'

With these and many other words of prayers, I put my petition before God.

My husband suggested we go to our family doctor to let him know what was going on. About a week later, armed with my scan result, we were off to Surulere, to see the doctor. It was about an hour's drive from where we lived, and so we had to leave early, to beat the traffic that was typical of that route.

The doctor listened intently as I explained what happened. Occasionally, he glanced at the scan result in his hands and nodded at intervals. There was silence after I stopped speaking. He checked the scan result again, going through it more intently. Suddenly, he looked up and gave me back the result. 'I would like you to do another scan in another lab,' he said.

Secretly, I wondered why there was a need for another scan, especially as he had confirmed that the first scan showed that the coil was lodged in the upper part of the womb. But I collected the referral letter to the lab he specified, went there, and did the scan.

As soon as we collected the scan result the following Tuesday, we went straight to the doctor.

Just like the last time, he checked the scan result, going through it intently. But this time, when he raised his head, he looked puzzled. 'I can't find the coil again,' he said.

'How was that possible? He probably didn't check it well,' I thought.

Well, he did check it again and again and the verdict still came out the same. The coil was no longer there.

The doctor decided to interrogate me. Was my menstrual flow usually heavy? I said 'Yes.' When did I have my last period? I replied that I just finished one. Was the flow heavy? I replied in the affirmative. He said that the coil might have been flushed out by my heavy period.

But the coil was already in the womb, how was the heavy

period going to flush it from there? He had no theory for that.

I wasn't buying it. First off, a heavy period couldn't flush out a coil that had already embedded itself in the womb. Secondly, how come it was between the first scan and the second scan that it was flushed out. The coil had been there all this while. Why was it now that it went out? Even the doctor himself was skeptical.

After debating the matter back and forth, we finally concluded that we needed a third opinion. This time we decided to go to the best lab in town, Mecure.

Mecure had sophisticated machines and had a reputation for accurate test results. The doctor recommended that we do both a scan and an x-ray, 'in case the coil had moved into any part of the body, the x-ray would pick it out,' he said.

Well, the following week, I went to Mecure, and the doctor asked me why I came for a scan. I told him my story and because of this, he did an extra check on me. He said he couldn't find anything. I went for the x-ray. The same thing, nothing! 'What kind of a miracle was this?' I wondered.

Long story short, I didn't go for the surgery, and till today there have been no issues. Praise the Lord!

CONCLUSION

It's been more than 21 years since I gave my life to Christ and I've never looked back or had cause to regret it. I had to learn a new way of life from the very beginning and because of this, I made my share of mistakes. But God saw the sincerity of my heart and my true repentance has always been so merciful to me. Trials and tribulations have come, but somehow, with His help, I have always overcome. Attacks have come from unimaginable quarters on many different levels and at different stages of my life. But guess what? God always fought for me - a former Islamic evangelist, an Arabic and Islamic scholar, and a Christian critic.

This book was written to encourage anyone who has gone through or is still going through life's troubles and trials and does not know where to turn. I encourage you to give your life to Jesus today!

Do not be like me who resisted Him until I had to submit at last. I wasted so many years going through needless heartaches and pain and shedding unnecessary tears when there was somebody just waiting to carry my burden for me.

Jesus said in Matthew 11:29-30: 'Take my yoke upon you, and learn of Me, for I am meek and lowly in heart and ye shall find rest for your souls. For My yoke is easy, and My burden is light.'

What is His yoke that He is asking you to take upon you? It is the yoke of taking that bold step to invite Jesus into your life as your Saviour and Lord. And what does He promise you thereafter? Rest for your souls? Isn't that fantastic?

So, my dear friend, what are you waiting for?

If you're ready to give your life to Jesus Christ, say after me:

Lord Jesus, I know that I am a sinner, and today I ask that You forgive me all my sins. I believe you died for my sins and rose from the dead. I turn from my sins and invite You to come into my heart and life. I want to follow You as my Saviour and my Lord. Amen.

Praise the Lord!

Today marks the beginning of a new dawn in your life.

Right now, the host of heaven is rejoicing that you have been translated from the Kingdom of darkness into God's marvelous light. Hallelujah!

I want you to look for a bible believing church around you and begin to attend. Also, make every effort to build a deeper relationship with God by reading your bible and praying often. May the Lord bless you, keep you and help you to uphold your faith in Him till the very end, AMEN.

ABOUT THE AUTHOR

Fatima experienced abuse, trauma, and abandonment right from her childhood up until adulthood, depicting what children from failed marriages and broken homes have to go through because of their parent's separation.

However, God turned it around for her salvation, deliverance, and healing

Soon after she gave her life to Christ, Fatima began to have angelic visitations and spiritual encounters. These encounters have had a profound impact on her life. She is living proof that no matter what anyone is going through in life, there is always hope at the end of the tunnel.

This is a story of hope, love, and faith.